Le Cordon Bleu

Techniques and Recipes

Poultry, Game & Eggs

Le Cordon Bleu

Techniques and Recipes

Poultry, Game & Eggs

Jeni Wright and Eric Treuille

CASSELL

A CASSELL BOOK

This edition first published in the United Kingdom in 1998 by
Cassell plc
Wellington House
125 Strand
London WC2R 0BB

Created and produced by
CARROLL & BROWN LIMITED
20 Lonsdale Road
London NW6 6RD

Material in this book has been previously published in
Le Cordon Bleu Complete Cooking Techniques
published by Cassell at £25

Copyright © 1996 Carroll & Brown Limited/Le Cordon Bleu BV

British Library Catalogue-in-Publication Data
A catalogue record for this book is available from the
British Library

ISBN 0-304-35122-9

Reproduced by Colourscan, Singapore
Printed and bound in Great Britain by Jarrold Book Printing,
Thetford, Norfolk

CONTENTS

CHOOSING POULTRY

Whether fresh or frozen, look for well-shaped plump birds that have blemish free, light, even-coloured skin. That of fresh birds should look moist but not wet; wetness can indicate the bird has been partially frozen. Feed and breed can affect the colour of the skin and the flavour of the meat.

MAKE SURE the legs are pliable and the skin intact

SELECT BIRDS with moist, even coloured skin, there should be no signs of bruising or feathers

WHEN SELECTING younger birds gently bend the tip of the breastbone, it should be flexible

THE BODY SHOULD be compact, well rounded in shape with plump, firm breasts

THE BIRD SHOULD smell fresh, any smells from the wrapping should disappear quickly

BUYING POULTRY

Most supermarket birds are conventionally reared and have a consistently bland taste. Free range birds, which are more expensive, are more flavourful as a result of their varied diet and free roaming conditions. The words "free range", "traditional free range" or "free range total freedom", on labels all indicate the birds have been allowed to grow in specially designed houses, however the number of birds per square metre varies.

When choosing frozen birds make sure the wrapping is sealed and intact and that there are no ice crystals or discoloration – a sign of freezer burn on the skin. Use the chart on the opposite page to select an appropriate bird for each occasion and to check the suitable cooking methods. When considering game, domestic rabbit is generally included with wild birds.

HANDLING POULTRY

Remove the original packaging from a fresh bird then place on a rack over a plate. Cover loosely and store in the refrigerator (1–5°C) away from cooked meats. Store any giblets separately in a covered bowl.

Always check the label on frozen birds and portions for freezer storage times. Frozen poultry must be defrosted completely before cooking. Thaw in the original packaging on a plate in the refrigerator allowing 3–5 hours per 450 g. Remove any giblets as soon as possible. Cook the bird within 12 hours of thawing and do not refreeze. Raw poultry is susceptible to bacterial growth so clean work surfaces and all preparation utensils after use. To store cooked poultry, cool it quickly then cover and store in the refrigerator for 2–3 days.

POULTRY & GAME

Chicken and turkey suit everyday and special occasion meals while other birds are generally reserved specially for the latter. Select young tender birds for quick cooking such as stir-frying and grilling and older birds for slow, moist methods, like stewing, which will help to tenderize the flesh and draw flavour from the bones. Ask your butcher for help with selection advice.

BIRD	WHAT TO LOOK FOR	COOKING METHODS
BOILING FOWL	*Lean breast with firm breastbone* *Slightly mottled skin* *Flesh a little darker than chicken*	Braise, stew, casserole, boil, poach, steam
CHICKEN	*Creamy-white smooth skin, should look fresh and moist*	Roast, pot-roast, braise, casserole, steam, poach, pan-fry, deep-fry, stir-fry
DUCK	*Supple, waxy looking skin* *Dry appearance* *Long body with slender breasts*	Roast (whole) Pan-fry, grill (breasts) Use fat for roasting potatoes
GOOSE	*Plump breast with flexible backbone* *Light coloured waxy skin* *Yellow fat in body cavity*	Roast, pot-roast Braise, stew (portions)
GROUSE	*Moist fresh-looking skin* *Deep red flesh, with no "shot" damage*	Roast, pot-roast, braise, casserole, stew
GUINEA FOWL	*Long lean breasts* *Golden skin and fat, dark coloured flesh*	Bard and roast, pot-roast, casserole
PARTRIDGE	*Plump, pale coloured, soft flesh* *Obvious gamey aroma*	Roast, pot-roast, braise, casserole, stew
PHEASANT	*Good even shape with no "shot" damage* *Limbs intact and not broken* *Strong gamey aroma*	Bard and roast, stew, braise
POUSSIN	*Moist creamy-white skin* *Plump legs and lean breasts*	Roast (whole) Grill, barbecue (spatchcock)
QUAIL	*High proportion of meaty flesh to bone* *Good round shape, plump flesh*	Roast, pot-roast, braise, casserole, grill, barbecue (spatchcock)
RABBIT	*Even covering of flesh and rounded back* *Lean, moist, pale pink flesh* *Very little visible fat*	Pan-fry, grill, roast, braise, stew, casserole
TURKEY	*Plump, well rounded breast and legs* *Moist skin with no blemishes* *Very little odour*	Roast (whole) Roast, braise, casserole (portions) Stir-fry, pan-fry (breast meat)

CHICKEN ON THE MENU

Inexpensive, easy to prepare and perfect with a vast range of seasonings and accompaniments, chicken is a popular dish practically everywhere.

CHINA – *Bang Bang Chicken* (shredded, poached chicken served with cucumber shreds and a spicy dressing) is a favourite appetiser dish.

EASTERN EUROPE – *Chicken Paprikash* (chicken pieces cooked in a tomato and paprika-flavoured sauce) is a Hungarian classic while *Chicken Pojarski* (deep-fried minced chicken and brioche balls in a tomato-mushroom sauce) was once a favourite of the Russian royal family.

FRANCE – *Coq au vin* is a slowly simmered chicken that gets its rich flavour from red wine, bacon and mushrooms.

GREAT BRITAIN – *Hindle Wakes* (chicken with a fruit, vinegar and mustard stuffing) is a time-honoured Yorkshire classic.

INDIA – *Tandoori Chicken* is marinated in spicy yogurt and cooked in a clay oven.

ITALY – *Chicken Cacciatore* (or "hunter's style") is made with a mushroom and wine-infused tomato sauce.

UNITED STATES – *Southern-fried Chicken* (chicken pieces dipped into seasoned flour and fried) is a picnic staple all over the country.

PREPARING WHOLE BIRDS

All birds, both domestic – chickens, ducks and geese – and game birds such as partridges or grouse, need careful preparation, not least because keeping the bird's shape during cooking makes carving easier. Before trussing, clean away feathers and down, rinse inside and out, and dry with paper towels.

GIBLETS

The giblets consist of the neck, gizzard, heart and liver of the bird as well as the lungs and intestines (though the last two are generally not included in ready-prepared birds). Unless you clean the bird yourself, you will usually find the giblets packed in a plastic bag inside the body cavity. Often, however, they are absent from ready-prepared birds. Occasionally, you can buy them separately from a butcher if you wish to prepare stock.

To make stock for gravy (see page 19), trim the giblets, discarding the membrane and yellow gall bladder from the liver. Simmer them with a few tablespoonfuls of chopped onion and carrot, a bouquet garni and a few black peppercorns.

The livers of poultry (see page 12) and some fresh game birds are delicious in their own right, although the giblets of well-hung game birds are best discarded.

Handle and cook giblets as you would poultry. Store them separately, in a covered container away from cooked meats, in the refrigerator for 1–2 days. Always cook thoroughly before eating.

REMOVING THE WISHBONE

The wishbone is located at the neck end of the bird. It is not necessary to remove it, but if you do it will be easier to carve the breast. This is particularly important if you are dealing with a large chicken or a turkey. Use a small pointed knife.

1 Pull back the skin from the neck cavity of the bird. Cut around the wishbone.

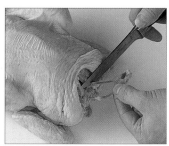

2 Scrape the meat from the wishbone, then cut away at the base.

TRUSSING SMALL BIRDS

Trussing gives the bird a neat shape and helps keep stuffing in place. Use a string to tie quite small birds, such as poussins, partridges, pheasants, grouse and quails, around their legs and bodies. Before you begin to tie up the birds, tuck the wing tips and the neck flap underneath.

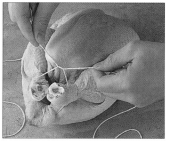

1 After seasoning, with the bird breast-side up, tie string around the legs and under the skin-flap at the tail.

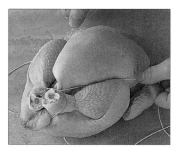

2 Bring the string towards the neck end of the bird, passing it down between the legs and body.

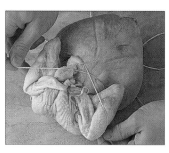

3 Turn the bird over. Cross the string over the centre of the bird. Wrap the string around the wings to keep them flat against the bird.

4 Pull the string to bring the wings together, and then tie a firm, double knot. The bird is now ready for cooking – roasting, pot-roasting, barbecuing or casseroling.

TRUSSING LARGE BIRDS

Trussing with a needle and thread is beneficial for large birds, and professional chefs always truss birds this way to ensure a neat, compact shape. Trussing helps the bird retain its natural juices, keeping the flesh moist and flavourful.

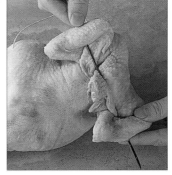

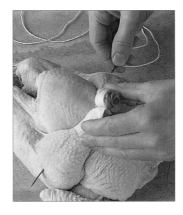

1 With the bird breast-side up, push the legs back to the centre of the breasts. Insert the needle through the joint in one of the legs, push it through the body, and out through the other leg. A 15-cm piece of string should remain where the needle first entered the bird.

2 Tuck the wing tips under the body, and fold over the flap of skin from the neck. Thread the string through the wings and flap of skin.

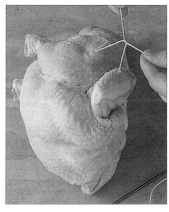

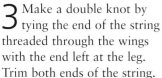

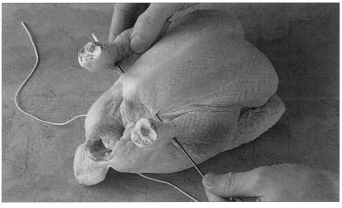

3 Make a double knot by tying the end of the string threaded through the wings with the end left at the leg. Trim both ends of the string.

4 Thread the needle under the legs through the tail end, leaving a 15-cm piece of string where the needle first entered the bird. Insert the needle through the end of one leg, push it through the breast, and out through the other leg.

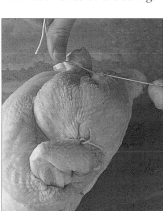

5 Make a double knot by tying the end of the string that has been threaded through the legs with the end left at the tail. Cut both ends of the string.

6 Turn the bird, breast-side up. It is now ready for cooking – roasting, pot-roasting, poaching or barbecuing (see pages 18, 28 and 31 respectively).

TRUSSING NEEDLE

To truss a large bird you need a special trussing needle. These are available in various lengths from specialist kitchenware shops. Make sure you use one which is long enough to pierce the bird fully through both legs and body. A small turkey, for example, will require a trussing needle of about 25 cm in length.

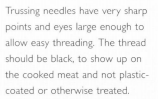

Trussing needles have very sharp points and eyes large enough to allow easy threading. The thread should be black, to show up on the cooked meat and not plastic-coated or otherwise treated.

TRICK OF THE TRADE
•

QUICK TRUSSING
Large birds that are to be roasted without a stuffing or barbecued can be quickly and simply secured by the insertion of two large metal skewers. One is pushed through both sections of the wing, into the neck skin and out through the other wing. The other skewer is pushed through the thighs and tail cavity. Thus secured, the bird will hold its shape and is ready for cooking.

JOINTING & CUTTING

Birds are usually left whole for roasting, pot-roasting and poaching, but for most other cooking methods they are cut up into pieces, unless they are small birds such as poussins or quail. The number of pieces depends on the size of the bird. Some small birds like pheasant, for example, may be spatchcocked or cut in half. Others are jointed into four, six or eight pieces.

SPATCHCOCKING

The derivation of this very strange-sounding culinary term is slightly obscure. An old word dating back to the 16th century, most likely of Irish origin, it is said to have come from the habit of catering for unexpected guests by speedily killing a bird and roasting it over the fire – "despatching the cock" – hence spatchcock. The word has now come to mean the cutting and removing of the backbone so that the bird can be cooked flat – and therefore more quickly.

SPATCHCOCKING A BIRD

Small birds such as the poussins used here are perfect for barbecuing or grilling. To make them the same thickness throughout so that they cook quickly and evenly, the backbone is removed, then the birds are flattened and secured with metal skewers – called en crapaudine *in French.*

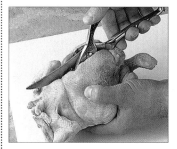  

1 Tuck under the wings and remove the wishbone. Turn the bird over, cut along each side of the backbone with poultry shears and remove it.

2 Push down on the bird to break the breastbone, flattening it against the cutting board.

3 Keeping the bird flat, push a metal skewer through the wings and breast. Push another metal skewer through the thighs.

CUTTING A DUCK INTO FOUR PIECES

Ducks are less economical than chickens, because they have less meat in proportion to their weight, and more fat stored under the skin. They are also a different, more awkward shape for jointing, and are therefore best cut into four pieces so that each portion contains a good amount of meat to bone. The joints can be roasted or casseroled.

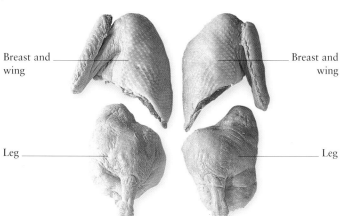

Breast and wing

Breast and wing

Leg

Leg

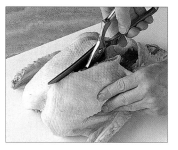 

1 Trim wing tips and remove wishbone (see page 8). Cut breast in half from tail to neck, splitting the breastbone with poultry shears.

2 Separate the bird into two halves by cutting along each side of the backbone and removing it.

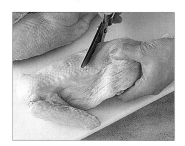

3 Cut each piece of duck diagonally in half with poultry shears. The duck is now ready for cooking.

CUTTING A BIRD INTO EIGHT PIECES

A medium-sized or large bird can be jointed into four, six or eight pieces. For some dishes you may wish to keep the breasts and/or the legs intact, but to ensure there is some white and dark meat for each serving, breasts are cut in half with the wings attached and the legs are split into thighs and drumsticks.

POULTRY SHEARS

Professional chefs joint poultry with a large knife, but for cutting the breastbone and backbone, you may find poultry shears easier.

Poultry shears have strong upward-curving blades, one with a straight edge and one with a serrated edge. Some have a notch in the lower blade which helps get a grip on bones. The handles are strongly sprung and are closed with a loop that holds the blades shut when not in use.

1 Place the bird breast-side up and cut one leg away from the bird. Cut through the thigh joint, to separate the leg from the body. Repeat.

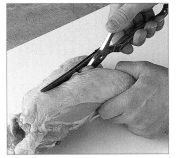

2 Holding the wing, cut the breast in half, splitting the breastbone. Turn over and cut alongside the backbone to separate the body.

3 Cut out the backbone with the poultry shears – it can be used to make stock. Leave the wing joints attached.

4 Cut each breast in half diagonally with the shears, so that one piece of breast has the wing attached.

5 Cut each leg in half through the knee joint, following the line of white fat on the underside. Cut off wing tip at first joint.

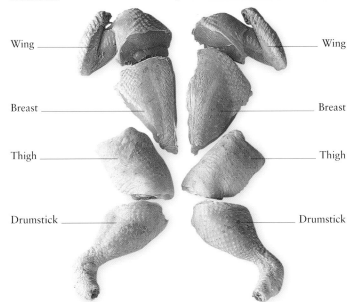

Wing   Wing

Breast   Breast

Thigh   Thigh

Drumstick   Drumstick

CUTTING UP A RABBIT

Rabbits can be roasted whole, but it is more usual to joint them for slow-cooking in casseroles and stews. It is only wild rabbit that you may need to joint, since domestic rabbit is mainly sold ready jointed. A whole rabbit, depending on size, can be jointed into six to nine pieces which will feed three to five people. Boneless rabbit meat is a good choice for pâtés and terrines (see page 34).

1 Cut the back legs from the carcass with a large chef's knife. Cut down the centre to separate. Cut each leg in two.

2 Cut the body crosswise into three or four pieces with the knife, making one cut below the ribcage.

3 Cut the rib section in half through the breastbone and backbone with the knife or kitchen scissors.

PREPARING PIECES

Poultry is immensely versatile: it can be cut into suprêmes and escalopes for pan-frying, chargrilling, stuffing and poaching as well as into strips for stir-frying. Thighs provide lean chunky pieces for casseroles and kebabs.

MAKING SUPREMES

These are skinless, boneless chicken breasts. Traditionally, they include the wing bones, but are often prepared without. Although available ready-prepared, preparation at home is more economical. Joint the bird (see page 11), cutting off both wings but keeping the breasts whole.

1 With your fingers, pull the skin and membrane away from the chicken breast. Discard skin and membrane.

2 Turn the breast over and cut away the rib cage. Remove the tendons from the breast (see below).

3 Turn the breast over, skinned-side up, and trim away fat and rough edges. The suprême is now ready.

PREPARING POULTRY & GAME LIVERS

Poultry livers and those of some fresh game birds can be gently sautéed and served on toast or with dressed salad leaves; they are also very good in pâtés and terrines.

Poultry livers consist of smooth lobes surrounded by membranes and sinews. Trim the livers, removing all tubes, membrane and fine, stringy sinews that would be unpleasant in the mouth. Remove the gall bladder and cut away any dark brown or yellowish patches around it.

REMOVING THE TENDONS

There are two tendons in a chicken breast, one in the small fillet and one in the main breast. Removing them is not essential, but it does make for easier slicing and eating. In step 2, the main sinew is removed prior to slicing strips for stir-frying.

1 Pull away the small fillet. Cut out the tendon with a chef's knife.

2 Cut away the tendon from the breast, using a cleaver or chef's knife.

MAKING ESCALOPES

A chicken breast provides two escalopes, a turkey breast, three or more. Escalopes can be pan-fried plain or coated (see page 26), chargrilled (see page 27), or made into pinwheels (see page 29).

1 Remove the skin and tendons (see above). Split in half horizontally with a knife.

2 Place each piece of chicken between two sheets of baking parchment. Pound all over with a rolling pin until flattened.

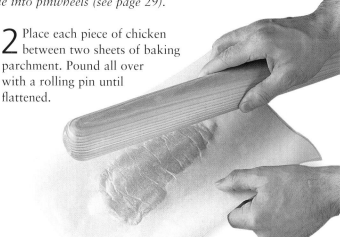

CUTTING POULTRY FOR STIR-FRYING

Poultry meat is ideal for stir-frying because it cooks rapidly, quickly becomes tender and marries well with the strong flavours of Asian cooking. Skinless, boneless breast of chicken, turkey and duck are most often used, and the strips marinated to heighten flavour. For the technique of stir-frying poultry, see page 27.

Trim the breasts of any fat and remove the tendons (see opposite page). Put the breasts between two sheets of baking parchment and pound with the flat side of a cleaver. Remove the paper and thinly slice the breasts, working diagonally across the grain of the meat (see box, right).

GOING AGAINST THE GRAIN

Meat that is cut "cross-grain" as the Chinese call it, has three advantages: a greater cut surface area is exposed to the heat making cooking very quick; long fibres are cut which makes the flesh more tender; and the strips hold their shape during cooking.

PREPARING THIGH MEAT FOR KEBABS

Thigh meat is good for kebabs as it is firmer than breast. A marinade adds flavour and moisture – soaked at least an hour before cooking, preferably overnight. Another trick is to leave the skin on for cooking, then remove it just before serving.

3 Marinate the meat if you like, then fold the pieces in half and thread on to skewers. Alternate the meat with cubed or sliced vegetables, to add colour and make the meat go further.

1 Remove the skin. Cut the flesh from one end of the thigh bone. Lift the bone and scrape away the flesh. Cut the bone from the meat.

2 Cut the thigh into large pieces, across the grain of the meat. Cut away any sinew or bone that may be attached to the meat.

PREPARING A WHOLE BREAST OF DUCK

The breasts are the best part of the duck. They are long, thick, meaty and boneless, and can be pan-fried, roasted, grilled or chargrilled whole and carved crosswise into neat, elegant slices to serve. The french word magret *is used to describe any duck breast, although it originally only related to Barbary duck. Breasts can be cut from a whole duck (before it is jointed) using a boning knife, or can be bought ready-cut. They are not usually skinned.*

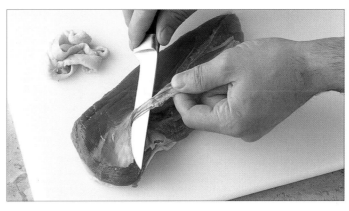

1 Trim away the rough edges of skin from the duck breast. Turn the breast on to its skin and trim away the tendon from the flesh with a boning knife.

2 Score a diamond pattern in the skin. This makes it more attractive for serving, and helps release fat during cooking (see page 26).

MAKING A BALLOTINE

The word ballotine comes from the French *ballot*, meaning bundle, a neat parcel of stuffing encased in lean, boneless poultry meat. Here, a whole bird is boned and then stuffed with a forcemeat mixture. Poultry breast meat or truffles are sometimes included in stuffings for ballotines, so too are whole or chopped nuts or stoned olives.

FORCEMEAT STUFFING

*350 g skinless boneless chicken
  breasts, cut into pieces*
60 g fresh breadcrumbs
2 tbsp milk
1 tbsp butter
1 shallot, chopped
1 garlic clove, chopped
1 egg white
*1 tbsp mixed fresh thyme
  and tarragon, chopped*
Salt and freshly ground pepper

Mince the chicken in a food processor or mincer and place in a bowl. Soak the breadcrumbs in the milk until it has been absorbed, then squeeze out the excess milk and add the bread to the chicken. Melt the butter in a pan and sauté the shallot and garlic until softened, about 5 minutes. Let cool, then add to the chicken and breadcrumbs and mix well. Bind the mixture with the egg white and then add the chopped herbs and salt and pepper to taste. Makes enough stuffing for a 1.25 kg bird.

BONING THE BIRD

Ballotines are usually made with duck, turkey or, as here, chicken, but game birds such as pheasant or grouse are also suitable. You can ask your butcher to bone the bird for you, or do it yourself following the techniques shown here. Reserve the carcass for stock. A ballotine is almost always served cold, so start making it the day before you wish to serve it to allow time for the meat to settle and cool after cooking.

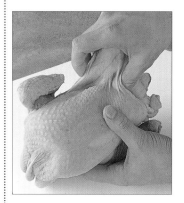

1 Dislocate each leg by breaking it at the thigh joint. Carefully remove the wishbone with a boning knife (see page 8).

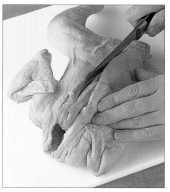

2 With the bird breast-side down on the cutting board, cut down the centre of the backbone from the neck to the tail end.

3 Working from the front of the bird to the back, carefully scrape away the flesh on one side of the backbone, cutting into the bird to expose the ribcage.

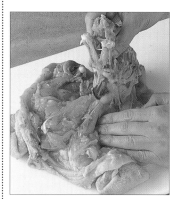

4 Repeat on the other side of the backbone, being careful not to pierce the breast skin with the knife. Pull the rib and backbone from the flesh of the bird.

5 Scrape away the flesh from each thigh bone and cut away the bone at the joint with a knife or poultry shears. Scrape all the flesh away from the wings up to the first joint.

6 Remove the exposed wing bone by cutting away the rest of the wing at the joint. Cut away the tendon from each fillet and breast. The chicken is now ready for stuffing and rolling.

STUFFING AND ROLLING

After careful boning and stuffing, the bird is rolled into a neat sausage shape, wrapped in baking parchment, and foil, then tied securely with string. This holds the meat and stuffing tightly and makes a neat shape for easy slicing.

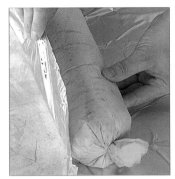

3 Dampen a large piece of baking parchment with water. Place the stuffed bird parallel to one long end of the paper, and roll the paper tightly around it, to make a cylinder. Twist the ends to seal. Place the wrapped bird on a large piece of foil and roll up in a similar way.

1 Season the inside of the whole boned bird with salt and pepper. Spread the stuffing (see page 14) evenly over the inside of the bird and pull up the sides of the bird to cover the stuffing.

2 Stitch the bird closed from the tail to neck end with a trussing needle (see page 9) and thread. Season the outside of the bird by rubbing the skin with salt and pepper.

4 Cut a piece of kitchen string about 1 metre long. Wrap the string first around the length of the cylinder, then several times around its width at regular intervals, securing the ends of the string with double knots.

POACHING AND SLICING

Ballotines are usually poached very slowly in water, stock or another flavoured liquid, then left overnight and served cold. Cooling the meat in its wrapping allows it to set in the cylinder shape and as a result makes slicing easier. Ballotines can also be braised on a bed of vegetables, in which case they are rolled and tied but left unwrapped and generally served hot.

1 Weigh the ballotine and calculate the cooking time, allowing 20 minutes per 450 g. Place in a pan, cover with stock and weight it down if necessary. Bring to the boil, then lower heat and poach for the calculated time.

2 Let the ballotine cool in the liquid. Lift out of the pan, cut string and unwrap. Snip one end of the thread and pull it out. Slice the ballotine and serve cold, with a garnish of your choice (see page 33).

Cailles Rôties Farcies Madame Brassart

*This wonderfully rich dish of stuffed quails is named after the founder of
Le Cordon Bleu, Madame Brassart. Boned quails, filled with a mixture of
wild rice, foie gras and ceps, are roasted and served with two sauces.*

SERVES 4

4 quails

*Goose fat or a mixture of
butter and oil*

*Salt and freshly ground
pepper*

FOR THE STUFFING

90 g wild rice

300 ml chicken stock

*100 g foie gras,
cut into small cubes*

*150 g fresh ceps,
cleaned and finely chopped*

2 shallots, finely chopped

*30 g mixed fresh herbs
(parsley, chervil, basil),
chopped*

1–2 tbsp port or cognac

*Pinch of quatre-épices or
ground mixed spice*

*Fresh parsley and rosemary,
to garnish*

Bone the quails whole (see box, below). Roast the carcasses at 200°C for 10 minutes, then use the bones to flavour the port sauce (see box, right).

Make the stuffing: simmer the rice in the stock for 30–40 minutes, until tender and set aside. Season the foie gras with salt and pepper and sauté in a hot frying pan until the cubes are sealed on all sides. Add to the rice.

Heat 1 tbsp goose fat in the frying pan and sauté the ceps until wilted. Add the shallots and herbs and sauté until the shallots are soft. Reserve a few ceps for garnish; add the rest to the rice with the port and spice. Check seasoning and let cool.

Season inside the quails; fill them loosely with stuffing and truss. Heat 3 tbsp goose fat in a roasting tin, and brown the quails on all sides. Roast the quails at 200°C for 15-20 minutes, basting occasionally. Remove from the oven and arrange the birds on a platter.

Reheat the port sauce and spoon some sauce around the quails. Garnish with parsley, rosemary and the reserved ceps. Serve crème d'ail (see box, below left) and remaining sauce separately.

PORT SAUCE

200 g shallots, sliced
60 g butter
4 roasted quail carcasses
50 ml sherry vinegar
250 ml port
750 ml chicken stock
I sprig of fresh thyme

Sweat the shallots in butter. Add the carcasses and vinegar and boil until almost evaporated. Stir in the port and reduce by half, then add the stock and thyme and simmer for 20 minutes. Strain and season to taste.

CREME D'AIL

I2 garlic cloves, peeled
200 ml double cream

Blanch garlic cloves, drain and refresh. Put in a pan with cream. Cook for 10 minutes until garlic is soft. Continue cooking until reduced by half, then purée in a blender. If too thick, thin with chicken stock. Check seasoning.

Boning a Quail Whole

This clever technique removes the carcass from a tiny bird so that the bird is left whole with its skin intact. When the bird is stuffed, it therefore retains its shape. Because quails are so tiny, use a small pointed knife and your fingertips.

Remove the wishbone (see page 8). Loosen the leg bones from the carcass. Cut the wings from the carcass.

Insert a small knife between the rib cage and the flesh and scrape all around to free the flesh from the carcass.

When the carcass is free, pull it out with your fingers and roast the bones for using in the port sauce.

ROASTING BIRDS

Use a roasting tin that is only a little larger than the bird and cook on a rack or a bed of vegetables to prevent it from being fried underneath. Cover large birds halfway through cooking to prevent overbrowning.

ROASTING TIMES

The following roasting times are approximate, so test for doneness (see page 19) to be absolutely sure the bird is properly cooked. Before cooking, weigh the bird and calculate the total cooking time.

- CAPON
  190°C for 25 mins per 450 g

- CHICKEN
  200°C for 18 mins per 450 g
  plus an extra 18 mins

- GUINEA FOWL
  200°C for 15 mins per 450 g
  plus an extra 15 mins

- POUSSIN
  200°C for 25–40 mins

- TURKEY
  180°C for 20 mins per 450 g
  under 4.5 kg
  16–18 mins per 450 g
  over 4.5 kg

ROASTING A WHOLE BIRD

Poultry and game birds have little natural fat, so to make sure the meat stays moist during roasting place fat on the skin before placing in the oven. Butter gives a good flavour and blends with sediment in the tin to make rich-tasting juices (jus in French) or gravy (see opposite page).

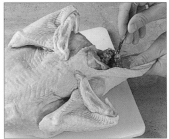

1 Wipe the bird inside and out with paper towels. Season the cavity and insert flavourings (see below, right).

2 With the bird breast-side down, season the neck end and spoon in stuffing if you like (see below left).

3 Tuck drumsticks under tail skin, put the bird on a rack in tin. Cover the breast generously with butter.

4 Roast the bird (see chart, left), basting frequently. Start cooking the bird on one of its sides for 15–20 minutes then turn it over and cook on the other side for the same length of time. Turn breast-side up for the remainder of the roasting time.

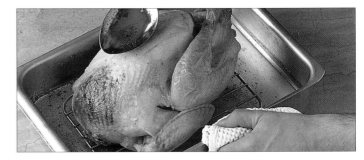

STUFFINGS FOR POULTRY

Sausagemeat, breadcrumbs and cooked rice are all good stuffing bases. Add seasonings and, for different textures, nuts and dried fruit. Prepare about 225 g for a 2.25 kg bird and chill for at least 2 hours. Loosely stuff the neck end. Stuffing the body cavity can prevent heat from penetrating the centre and is not recommended for large birds. Stuff the bird shortly before you roast it, letting it come to room temperature to ensure even cooking.

For a tasty meaty stuffing, mix sausagemeat, chopped onion, nuts, parsley, raisins, apricots and breadcrumbs. Bind with egg and season.

KEEPING POULTRY MOIST

When roasting any bird, but especially the drier kind like turkey and pheasant, it is important to keep the meat as moist as possible. Placing softened butter under the skin can help, or you can cover the bird loosely with buttered paper or foil. To brown the skin, remove the paper or foil for the last 20–30 minutes of cooking time. You can also cover the breast with streaky bacon (see page 21) or with back fat, as the French do.

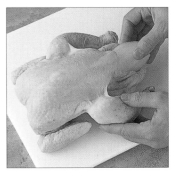

Another method to help keep a bird moist during roasting is to insert half an onion or a lemon wedge inside the cavity of the bird before roasting.

TESTING FOR DONENESS

After roasting a bird for the recommended time, always check it is properly cooked.

Hold the bird above the tin. If the juices run clear, not pink, it is fully cooked.

CUTTING UP A ROASTED BIRD

Before cutting up small and medium-sized birds, let them rest for about 15 minutes under a loose tent of foil so the meat can relax and the juices settle. This will make carving easier. After resting, remove any trussing string and cut up the bird using a large chef's knife or carving knife. A two-pronged fork can be used to steady the bird.

1 Place the bird breast-side up. Cut each leg from the bird and then in half to separate the drumstick and thigh, following the line of white fat on the underside.

2 Hold the bird steady on the cutting board with a two-pronged fork. Carefully cut the breast in half by splitting the soft breastbone and backbone.

3 Cut each breast piece in half diagonally, leaving a good part of the breast meat attached to the wing. Arrange the pieces on a warmed serving platter.

CARVING A ROASTED BIRD

Turkeys and large chickens are best served with their meat carved into neat slices. Before carving let the bird rest, as above, then snip away any trussing string and then carve. The dark meat can also be sliced from the drumstick, if you like.

1 Remove the legs, cut them in half and transfer to a warmed platter. Hold the bird steady with a fork and make a horizontal cut into the breast above the wing, cutting all the way to the bone.

2 Carve neat, even slices from the breast, holding the knife parallel to the ribcage. Repeat on the other side.

3 Arrange the slices of white meat, overlapping, on the platter with the drumsticks and thighs.

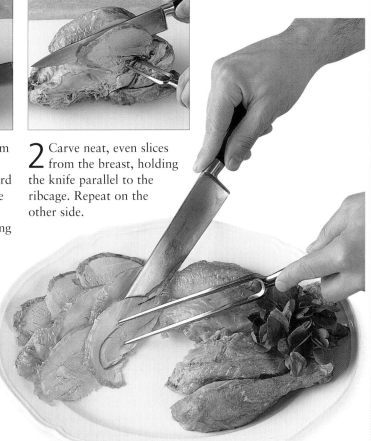

MAKING GRAVY

In France the juices (jus) from the tin are served with the bird; here they are thickened to make gravy.

Remove the bird from the tin and pour off all but about 1 tbsp fat. Put the tin over a low heat, sprinkle in 1 tbsp plain flour and stir well.

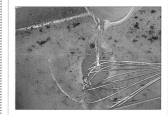

Gradually whisk in 500 ml hot stock or water. Increase the heat and bring to the boil. Simmer, whisking, for 1–2 minutes. Check seasoning. Serves 6–8.

PREPARING A FATTY BIRD FOR ROASTING

When roasting a fatty bird such as a duck (shown here) or goose, remove as much fat as possible beforehand and place the bird on a rack so that it does not sit in melted fat during roasting. Cooking times are given in the chart, left.

1 With bird breast-side up, cut away excess fat from tail and tail cavity. Remove the wishbone (see page 8).

2 Season inside the tail cavity with salt and pepper, then insert 1–2 bay leaves and a wedge of orange.

3 Place the bird breast-side up on a rack in a roasting tin. Pierce the bird all over with a metal skewer.

ROASTING AND CARVING DUCK

Weight for weight, duck serves less people than chicken but, because of its rich flavour, portions can be smaller. Small roast ducks are difficult to carve; they are best cut into four pieces as for an uncooked bird (see page 10).

1 Roast the bird (see chart, above left) first on one of its sides, then on the other. Turn it breast-side up for the remainder of the time until the juices from the thickest part of a leg run clear. Let the duck rest, loosely covered with foil, for 15 minutes.

2 Place the duck breast-side up and cut the legs from the bird with a large chef's knife or carving knife. Cut down through the thigh joints, to separate the legs from the body. Cut each wing away from the body of the duck at the shoulder joint.

3 On the main body of the bird, cut away one side of the breast meat in slices, moving inwards towards the breastbone. Repeat on the other side of the breast. Arrange the sliced breast, legs and wings on a warmed serving platter.

PREPARING AND ROASTING A GAME BIRD

The meat of young game birds is very lean and therefore tends to dry out easily during roasting. Barding the bird with fatty bacon helps make the flesh moist and flavoursome. A simple recipe for roast pheasant, using the techniques shown here, is given in the box, right.

1 Remove the wishbone (see page 8) before roasting so that the breast of the bird will be easy to carve.

2 Trim the wings by cutting through the second joint. Rinse the cavity, then wipe dry with paper towels. Truss the bird (see page 8).

3 Season the skin if you like, then cover loosely with bacon rashers around the breast and thighs.

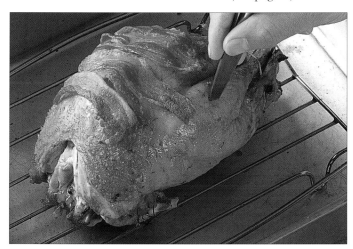

4 Roast the bird (see chart, opposite page) until the juices from the thickest part of a leg run clear, and the tip of a knife feels warm to the touch when withdrawn. Leave to rest, covered loosely with foil, for 10–15 minutes before carving.

ROAST PHEASANT WITH WINE GRAVY

1 kg pheasant
Salt and freshly ground pepper
3–4 streaky bacon rashers
2 tsp plain flour
300 ml red wine

Prepare the pheasant for roasting (see steps 1–3, left), then place on a rack in a roasting tin. Roast at 230°C for 10 minutes, then at 200°C for 30 minutes.

Remove the bird, cover loosely with foil and let rest for 10–15 minutes. Place the tin on top of the stove. Sprinkle in the flour, stir over a low heat for 2 minutes, then gradually whisk in the wine. Increase the heat and bring to the boil, then simmer, whisking, until thickened. Check seasoning. Serve the pheasant hot, with the gravy and accompaniments (see box, below). Serves 2.

ACCOMPANIMENTS FOR GAME BIRDS

There are many traditional accompaniments for game birds, and these are given in the box on page 22. Here are some additional ideas that can be used as well, to highlight the texture and flavour of the bird.

- Glazed carrot bâtons.
- Roast parsnips.
- Bunches of fragrant fresh herbs.
- Watercress bundles.
- Braised sliced red cabbage, onion and apple with port.

FINISHING TOUCHES

Use fruit and vegetables to complement the rich flavours of poultry and game dishes, as well as adding visual appeal to the presentation. Saucy dishes, such as casseroles and stews, are best served with croûtes, which will absorb the flavourful juices.

CLASSIC GARNISHES FOR GAME

Wild game is available during limited seasons, making it ideal for special occasions. These are the traditional accompaniments:

FRIED STRAW POTATOES: Very thin sticks of potato, called *pommes pailles* in French, deep-fried until crisp.

FRIED BREADCRUMBS: An English garnish.

CROUTES: Can be fried or toasted. For extra flavour, spread croûtes with smooth liver pâté before topping with small birds, such as woodcock or grouse

BREAD SAUCE: An English sauce made with bread, butter, cream, onions, milk and seasonings.

CUMBERLAND SAUCE: A fruity sauce made of redcurrant jelly, port, orange and lemon zest and juice, traditionally spiked with cinnamon or ginger and mustard.

TURNED MUSHROOMS
Trim stalk. Cut channels from centre of cap to edge. Use the knife tip to shape the top into a star.

HERBY HEARTS
Brush corners of heart-shaped croûtes with water and press very finely chopped parsley on to them.

GHERKIN FANS
Make thin lengthwise cuts in gherkins, leaving stalk ends intact. Fan out by pressing with your finger.

PEPPER TWISTS
Make two parallel cuts in a square of pepper, leaving opposite ends of the two cuts intact. Lift cut ends and twist.

TOMATO ROSES
Cut a long and continuous strip of of tomato skin in a spiral with a sharp knife. Roll up to form a rose.

CUCUMBER CHEVRONS
Quarter cucumber lengthwise; cut into chunks. Cut two V-shaped wedges in flesh, one deeper than the other; fan out.

CARROT BLOSSOMS
Cut lengthwise grooves in a carrot. Make angled cuts around end. Twist off; repeat. Fill each with a pepper dot.

VEGETABLE BUNDLES
Tie steamed asparagus tips together in bundles with a long strip of blanched and refreshed leek skin.

HOT BERRIES
Place halved strawberries and whole raspberries on a baking sheet and grill until lightly browned, 2–3 minutes.

GLAZED APPLES
Sprinkle unpeeled yellow apple slices with caster sugar, then grill until golden and bubbling, 2–3 minutes.

CHICORY BOATS
Separate chicory leaves and spoon a little peeled, deseeded and chopped tomatoes into the base of each leaf.

BITTER SHREDS
Use a sharp knife to cut purple chicory into fine strips. Or, as an alternative, use vibrant red radicchio.

FRIED FLOWERS
Deep-fry dry courgette flowers in 180°C oil until lightly browned, 15 seconds. Remove and drain on paper towels.

CARAMELIZED ORANGES
Briefly cook orange slices in a heavy sugar syrup until caramelized. Remove and garnish with parsley.

NUTTY FIGS
Make fig flowers by cutting a deep cross shape and fill each with half a walnut. Put under a hot grill for 2–3 minutes.

POACHED PEARS
Slice tops off poached pears at an angle. Remove core with a melon baller. Fill with redcurrant jelly. Replace tops.

CHAUDFROID DE CANARD

Coat duck slices with liquid aspic (see page 35) three times, chilling between each coating. Flood a platter with a layer of aspic; chill. Arrange orange wedges; flood and chill. Decorate the duck and arrange on the platter.

1 Cut thin strips of orange zest with a canelle knife and blanch; refresh and dry.

2 Pipe pâté on duck. Decorate with orange zest and coat with liquid aspic.

ORIENTAL ROAST DUCK

Based on Chinese tradition, a duck is often hung to dry, glazed and then roasted. Peking duck with its crispy, lacquered skin is the most famous example of this roasting method. There are various stages to the technique.

MAKING CHINESE SEASONING MIX

An aromatic mixture of garlic, ginger, chillies and spring onions is combined with spices and herbs to impart a delicate Oriental flavour to roast duck.

Heat a wok until hot. Add 2 tsp vegetable oil and heat until hot but not smoking. Add 3 finely chopped garlic cloves, 1 tbsp crushed fresh root ginger, 2 finely chopped and seeded fresh red chillies and 2 sliced spring onions and stir-fry until fragrant and just soft, about 2 minutes. Add 2 tsp toasted and crushed Sichuan peppercorns, 2 tbsp each yellow bean sauce and soy sauce and stir-fry to mix, then remove from the heat and let cool. Stir in 2 tbsp chopped fresh coriander just before applying to the skin of the bird to be roasted.

PREPARING THE DUCK

Before roasting, boiling water is poured over the duck. This tightens the skin and seals the pores so that the skin will be crisp when cooked.

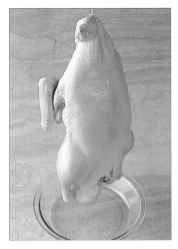

1 Trim away the excess fat from the tail end of the duck. Cut a long piece of kitchen string and tie it in a double knot around the fat at the neck end of the duck.

2 Bring about 2 litres water to the boil in a wok. Hold the duck in the water and ladle it over the duck until the skin becomes taut. Remove the duck and pat dry.

3 Hang the duck over a dish to catch the drips. Leave in a cool (10°C), airy place until the skin is dry, about 3 hours.

ROASTING THE DUCK

Once the duck is dried, the cavity is stuffed with Chinese seasoning mix and the skin is basted with maltose mixed with water. During roasting the flesh of the bird will take on the flavour of the Chinese seasoning and the skin will become crisp and dark in colour.

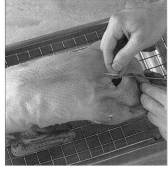

1 Soak a bamboo skewer in water for 30 minutes. Cut the string from the air-dried duck. Put the duck on a rack over a roasting tin. Spoon Chinese seasoning mix (see box, left) into the body cavity.

2 Thread the soaked bamboo skewer through the skin at the tail end of the duck to ensure that it remains closed while cooking. Roast the duck in a 200°C oven for 15 minutes.

3 Remove the duck from the oven and brush with maltose (see opposite page) and water. Lower the heat to 180°C and continue to roast, basting every 15 minutes, until the duck is dark brown, 1½–1¾ hours.

CARVING THE DUCK

This is the classic Chinese method for carving roast duck. The pieces are reassembled on the serving plate in the shape of the bird. Garnish with sprigs of fresh coriander, if you like.

This dark syrupy sugar solution is made from the fermented grains of barley, wheat or millet in a process sometimes called malting. It has been produced in China since the 2nd century BC and is commonly used in Chinese cooking for darkening the skin of roasted poultry and meat. Kept sealed, it will last indefinitely. Look for it at Oriental stores and large supermarkets.

To use it for Oriental roast duck, mix 1 tbsp maltose with 4 tbsp boiling water. If maltose is not available, you can use molasses instead.

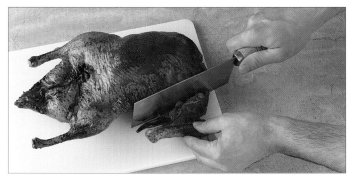

1 Let the duck rest for 15 minutes to allow the meat to retain its moisture and then place, with the breast-side up, on a cutting board. Carefully remove the bamboo skewer from the tail-flap. Cut each wing away from the body at the shoulder joint with a cleaver or large chef's knife. Cut each wing in half at the middle joint.

2 Remove each leg from the bird, cutting down through the thigh joint with a cleaver to separate it from the body. Cut the thigh from the drumstick at the joint between them.

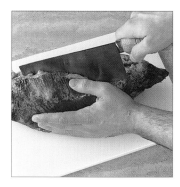

3 Turn the duck on its side and cut away the whole breast from the body, cutting through the rib bones and leaving the backbone behind. Cut the backbone and the meat still attached to it across into pieces.

4 Cut the breast in half lengthwise, splitting the breastbone with the cleaver. The breastbone is quite soft and splits easily.

5 Cut each half-breast across into roughly equal pieces, cutting down through the breastbone.

6 Arrange the meat on a warmed platter in the shape of the duck, starting with the wings, thighs, and drumsticks. Pile the pieces of back on top, followed by the pieces of breast.

FRYING

Pieces of poultry and game can be pan-fried, deep-fried, sautéed or stir-fried. These are all quick-cooking methods so small joints or breasts are the most suitable. The pieces can be fried plain, coated or stuffed.

PAN-FRYING A BREAST OF DUCK

Duck breasts can be "dry-fried" in their own fat and juices because they are so fatty. For successful results, trim and score the fat first (see page 13). Begin skin-side down, in a dry pan over a moderate heat, so the fat runs into the pan.

1 Season the duck breast and place skin-side down, in a frying pan. Cook for 3–5 minutes, pressing with a palette knife to extract the juices and keep the breast flat.

2 Turn the breast and cook for another 3–5 minutes (duck breast is best medium rare). Remove from the pan and let rest, covered. With the skin-side up and knife at a slant, cut thin diagonal slices.

MAKING SCHNITZELS

Escalopes cut from the breast (see page 12) can be pan-fried plain or coated with seasoned flour. Coating them in egg and breadcrumbs protects the delicate flesh. If you refrigerate them, uncovered, for one hour before pan-frying, the coating will harden to give a crisper result.

1 Season each escalope; dip in flour and beaten egg, then coat in fresh or dried breadcrumbs, pressing them firmly on to the meat.

2 Make criss-cross scores on the escalope with the back of a chef's knife. Heat enough oil and butter in a frying pan to just cover the bottom.

3 When the butter is foaming add the escalope. Cook over a moderate heat for 2–3 minutes on each side. Drain on paper towels. Serve.

STUFFING AND FRYING A CHICKEN BREAST

Boneless chicken breasts make perfect pockets for holding stuffings. Butter or soft cheese mixed with crushed garlic and/or herbs is the classic stuffing; chopped mushrooms, garlic and fresh herbs also work well, so too do chopped spinach and ricotta. Take care not to overfill the pocket or it may burst during cooking. The parcels can be fried plain or coated as for schnitzels above.

1 Cut a pocket 3–4 cm deep in the side of the breast, without puncturing the base of the pocket. Fill with stuffing.

2 Secure the opening by threading a soaked wooden cocktail stick through the cut edges of the breast.

3 Heat a little olive oil in a non-stick frying pan – just enough to cover the bottom of the pan. Add the parcels and cook, turning once, until golden on both sides, about 15 minutes. Remove the cocktail sticks before serving.

CHARGRILLING ESCALOPES

One of the simplest ways to fry escalopes is on a ridged cast-iron stovetop grill pan. The ridges on the pan give the meat a striped "chargrilled" effect, which looks most attractive and as if the meat has been barbecued. The escalopes are best simply fried in a good-quality virgin olive oil or a nut oil, or a mixture of oil and butter if you like. Deglazing the pan with balsamic vinegar adds to the flavour and is one of the simplest ways to make an instant sauce.

1 Brush a little olive oil over the pan and heat until hot but not smoking. Add the escalopes and cook over a moderate heat for 5 minutes, turning once. Add 1–2 tbsp balsamic vinegar and stir into the pan juices to make a tasty sauce.

2 Serve the escalopes on a bed of crisp rocket, as shown here, or on other leaves such as baby spinach or oak-leaf lettuce. Spoon the pan juices over the top of the escalopes and salad leaves as a dressing.

SAUTEING PIECES

Sautéing is the technique of turning joints or pieces in a pan over a high heat to seal and brown the skin. Turning prevents the meat from burning on the outside before the inside is properly cooked. Use a good-quality virgin olive oil or a mixture of oil and butter. Duck can be sautéed in its own fat.

In a flameproof casserole or sauté pan, heat about 2 tbsp oil to a high heat. Add the poultry pieces and cook until they begin to brown, turning them frequently with a fork or tongs to ensure they colour evenly. Reduce the heat to moderate and cook for 25–30 minutes or until done – the juices should run clear.

STIR-FRYING STRIPS OF POULTRY

Cut skinless, boneless breasts of chicken, turkey or duck across the grain into strips (see page 13). Coat and stir-fry as shown here, then stir-fry vegetables, liquid and flavourings in the wok according to your chosen recipe. Finally return the strips to the wok and toss with the other ingredients.

1 Stir the poultry strips in a mixture of egg white and cornflour until evenly coated. For 250 g chicken use 1 egg white and 1 tbsp cornflour, mixed until smooth.

2 Heat a wok until hot. Add 2 tbsp vegetable oil and heat until hot but not smoking. Add the poultry. Toss over a moderate to high heat for 5 minutes, or until tender. Remove with a slotted spoon.

POACHING

A whole chicken poached in a flavoursome broth is one of the most delicate dishes. You can also poach chicken breasts or thighs, with or without stuffing. Poached chicken meat is perfect for pie fillings and sandwiches.

POACHING A WHOLE BIRD

Gentle poaching is one of the classic ways of cooking a chicken. It leaves the meat tender and juicy, and produces a delicious broth. Trussing the chicken first (see page 8) ensures it retains its shape during cooking, while the weight of the bird determines the poaching time – allow 20 minutes per 450 g, poaching over a gentle heat on top of the stove.

1 Truss the chicken, including the neck end if you like, and place in a large pan. Pour over enough cold water to just cover the chicken. Bring the liquid slowly to the boil over a moderate heat.

2 Skim the surface with a slotted spoon. Lower the heat and add sliced carrots, onions and a bouquet garni. Poach, partially covered, for the calculated cooking time.

3 When the chicken is tender, remove from the poaching liquid, holding it over the pan so that as much liquid as possible drains from the bird. Remove the trussing string and cut the chicken into pieces (see page 10). Use the poaching liquid as a basic chicken stock or reduce and thicken to make a sauce.

SHREDDING POACHED POULTRY

The firm breast meat is best suited to this technique. Remove the breasts from the carcass while still warm – they will come away more easily. Begin shredding at the tip of the breast and work along to the other end, using a fine-pronged large fork.

Place the chicken breast-side up on a cutting board and pull off the skin. Remove the breasts from the carcass and shred the meat with the prongs of a fork. Remove the leg and wing meat from the carcass with your fingers; use as bite-sized pieces or shred if you like.

POULE AU POT

A whole poached chicken was the favourite dish of the French king, Henri Navarre, so much so that he wished his subjects could eat it on every Sunday of the year. *Poule au pot* is now one of the great classics of French cooking, and there are many regional variations. It may be stuffed with a mixture of breadcrumbs, sausagemeat and its own chopped liver, or with tarragon and lemon, or with truffles under the skin.

Henri Navarre (1553–1610)

SHREDDED POULTRY

Shredded poultry absorbs flavours and combines well with many flavoursome ingredients.

- Add to béchamel sauce, chill, then fill crêpes. Bake, topped with grated Parmesan.
- Mix shredded chicken or duck with sliced spring onion, grated ginger and soy sauce. Use to fill filo bundles or Chinese wontons.
- Serve shredded poultry on a bed of salad leaves, spoon over warm chilli and garlic dressing and top with croûtons.

POACHING PINWHEELS

This clever technique is surprisingly simple – chicken breasts are cut open, then rolled around a filling. After cooking, the rolls are sliced crosswise to reveal pinwheel shapes. For the filling, choose colourful and juicy ingredients, such as pepper strips, spinach, herbs and soft cheese. Here the rolls are foil-wrapped and poached; they can be wrapped in bacon and roasted.

THE ASIAN ALTERNATIVE

Asian chefs often prefer to retain the succulence of chicken breasts by poaching or steaming them in wrappers that also enclose flavour-imparting ingredients, such as lemon grass stalks.

1 Cut through one long side of a skinless, boneless chicken breast, leaving it attached on the opposite side. Detach the fillet and set aside.

2 Open the breast out flat, cut-side up. Put it between two sheets of baking parchment and pound with a rolling pin or meat mallet to flatten and stretch it. Remove the top sheet of parchment. Spread your chosen stuffing (in this case goat's cheese and chopped spinach) evenly over the cut side.

1 Cut a banana leaf into four squares, each one large enough to envelop a chicken breast. Brush each centre with a 1:1 hoisin and soy sauce mix. Place a chicken breast on each and top with lemon grass and a few slices of fresh root ginger. Spoon over more soy sauce.

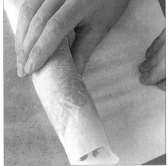

3 Replace the fillet in the centre of the breast, parallel to the long sides. Starting from one long side, roll the meat into a cylinder.

4 Roll the paper around the cylinder, pulling it tightly as you go, and twist the ends to seal. Wrap in foil and twist the ends as before.

5 Bring a pan of water to the boil and add the roll. Poach, covered, over a gentle heat for 15 minutes or until a metal skewer feels warm when withdrawn from the centre. Remove from the pan, unwrap and slice crosswise on the diagonal.

2 Wrap each leaf square around the chicken breast to make a neat parcel and secure with string if necessary. Place 1–2 packages at a time in a steamer basket over simmering water and cook for 15 minutes. Serve the chicken breasts in their banana leaves to be unwrapped at the table.

GRILLING & BARBECUING

The intense dry heat of both grill and barbecue crisps poultry skin and imparts a unique flavour. Small pieces, joints or whole birds can be cooked this way. For juiciest results, leave them unskinned or marinate before cooking.

MARINADES

- For a hot and spicy flavour, mix together crushed chillies, chopped fresh rosemary and garlic, and olive oil.
- Flavour plain, yogurt with Indian curry paste and chopped fresh coriander. For a Thai alternative, use green or red curry paste with the yogurt.
- To create a Mediterranean taste, combine olive oil, crushed garlic, and chopped fresh herbs.

CHICKEN SATE

4 skinless boneless chicken breasts
1 small onion, grated
2 garlic cloves, crushed
2 tbsp soy sauce
2 tbsp vegetable oil
2 tsp sugar
1 tbsp chopped fresh coriander
1 tsp turmeric
Peanut sauce, for serving

Slice the chicken into strips across the grain and mix with the onion, garlic, soy sauce, oil, sugar, coriander and turmeric. Cover and leave to marinate in the refrigerator overnight. Thread the strips on to soaked bamboo skewers and grill or barbecue for only 5 minutes, turning them frequently and brushing with the marinade. Serve hot, accompanied by peanut sauce. Serves 4–6.

GRILLING DRUMSTICKS

The meat of chicken drumsticks is especially suited to the grill or barbecue because it stays moist and tender even when cooked by intense heat. Using an oily marinade prevents the drumsticks from sticking to the rack. Cook slowly until the skin is crisp and golden.

1 Brush drumsticks all over with marinade (see box, left). You can slash the skin to help the marinade penetrate the meat. Cover and refrigerate for 1 hour.

2 Put the drumsticks on the rack of the grill pan and cook under a hot grill, about 6 cm away from the heat, for 15–20 minutes. Turn and baste frequently.

MAKING SATE

Saté are small kebabs made with very lean chicken, meat or fish. Here they are made with succulent chicken breast meat. The secret of making good chicken saté is to wind the chicken on to the sticks and not to overcook it or it will be dry. A simple recipe for chicken saté, using the techniques shown here, is given in the box, left.

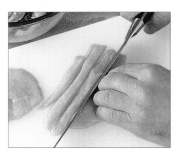

1 Remove the tendons from the chicken breasts (see page 12), then cut the flesh into thin slices, working diagonally across the grain. Marinate the strips for 1 hour, preferably overnight.

2 Soak bamboo skewers in water for 30 minutes, then drain. Thread the marinated chicken on to the skewers, winding them in a spiral pattern.

3 Cook the chicken under a very hot grill, about 6 cm away from the heat. The chicken will cook very quickly, so do not cook for longer than stated in the recipe. Turn the skewers frequently and brush with the marinade. Serve warm or at room temperature.

BARBECUING A WHOLE BIRD

A kettle barbecue allows you to cook a bird whole. This type of barbecue has a domed lid or hood which closes over the bird, in effect roasting it but with a chargrilled flavour.

1 Season the bird and place, uncovered, on a rack in a roasting tin. Place the tin on the barbecue grid and cover with the kettle lid.

2 Barbecue the chicken until the juices run clear (see page 19), allowing 1½–1¾ hours for a 2 kg bird. Lift the lid of the barbecue occasionally during cooking, and baste with the juices that have collected in the tin.

(see page 19)

BARBECUE TIPS

Outdoor cooking is quick, but requires constant attention. Prepare all your accompaniments in advance.

- Always barbecue outside – charcoal gives off carbon monoxide fumes.
- Light the barbecue at least 30 minutes before cooking and don't put food on it until the flames have died down and the coals have turned grey or are glowing embers.
- For extra flavour, strew the coals with woody herbs, such as rosemary, or fennel stems
- For safety's sake, use long tongs rather than ordinary kitchen forks to turn the food.

GRILLING A BIRD

Grilling or barbecuing is an ideal method for small birds such as poussins because they cook quickly and remain tender and moist. They cook faster when spatchcocked (see page 10), and have juicier flesh if marinated or their skins rubbed with olive oil and seasonings.

(see page 10)

1 Mix together the marinade ingredients of your choice (see box, opposite page). Put the bird in a non-metallic dish and prick all over with a fork. Pour over the marinade, cover and let marinate in the refrigerator for at least 4 hours, preferably overnight.

2 Preheat the grill until very hot. Put the spatchcocked bird, skin-side up, on the rack of the grill pan and grill about 7.5 cm from the heat for 30–40 minutes, turning frequently and occasionally brushing with the marinade.

3 Remove the bird from the rack and place on a cutting board. Remove the hot skewers with the help of a fork and a tea towel. Cut the bird in half lengthwise to serve, allowing one half per person.

CASSEROLING & POT-ROASTING

These are long, slow-cooking methods that give depth of flavour and unrivalled tenderness to any type of poultry or game, both whole birds and pieces on the bone. Cooking can be on top of the stove or in the oven.

COQ AU VIN

1 whole chicken, cut into 6 serving pieces (see page 11)
4 tbsp vegetable oil
1 tbsp plain flour
250 g carrots, sliced
1 onion, chopped
2 bay leaves
Salt and freshly ground pepper
175 g mushrooms, sliced

MARINADE
700 ml red wine
1 carrot, chopped
1 onion, chopped
2 garlic cloves, chopped
1 bouquet garni
4–5 juniper berries
1 tsp whole black peppercorns
200 ml red wine vinegar

Cook marinade ingredients, except vinegar, for 15 minutes. Transfer to a bowl and let cool. Stir in the vinegar; add the chicken. Sprinkle over half the oil, cover and refrigerate overnight.

Remove the chicken and strain the marinade. Heat the remaining oil in a flameproof casserole, add the chicken. Sauté until brown. In another pan, boil the marinade. Skim any blood from the surface.

Sprinkle the chicken with flour, add the remaining ingredients and stir over a moderate heat for a few minutes. Add the marinade and bring to the boil. Cook in a 180°C oven for 1 hour or until tender. Add the mushrooms for the last 15 minutes. Check seasoning. Serves 4–6

MARINATING AND CASSEROLING IN WINE

Poultry pieces are tenderized by being steeped and slowly simmered in a concentrated cooked red wine marinade. This is the technique behind the classic French coq au vin *(see box, left). For a fuller flavour, let the casserole go cold, preferably overnight. Reheat well before serving.*

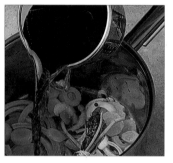

1 Cook the vegetables for the marinade in wine so that they will soften and impart flavour.

2 Let the chicken cool before adding to the marinade or the chicken will begin to cook before marinating.

3 Sprinkle oil over the surface of the marinade to help contain strong odours during marinating.

4 Make sure the chicken pieces are thoroughly dry before adding them to the hot oil otherwise they will not brown evenly.

5 Add the strained marinade to the casserole after it has been boiled and skimmed; this will have eliminated any coagulated blood.

6 When the chicken is done, the sauce will be thick and rich and the chicken will feel tender when pierced with a skewer. Let stand for 10–15 minutes before serving, to allow the flavours to mellow and the fibres in the meat to settle.

POT-ROASTING TOUGH GAME BIRDS

Small game birds, such as quail and grouse, can be dry and tough, so they are suited to slow, moist methods of cooking. Wrapping the birds in bacon adds flavour and protects the flesh; tying helps to keep the birds in a neat shape. Marinating before cooking (see box, right) will help moisten, flavour and tenderize the flesh.

1 Tuck the neck skin and wings underneath the birds and tie the legs together with string. Season the birds, then wrap streaky bacon rashers around them and tie it in place with kitchen string.

2 Heat 2 tbsp oil in a large flameproof casserole. Brown the birds, turning them occasionally by hooking a two-pronged fork under the trussing string.

3 Add carrots and onions to the pan, with salt and pepper to taste. Sweat the vegetables for 5 minutes over a gentle heat, stirring with a wooden spoon to incorporate any sediment from the bottom of the pan.

4 Pour enough red wine to half cover the birds. Cover and simmer very gently until the birds are tender and the sauce reduced, about 30 minutes on the stovetop, or 1 hour in a 180°C oven. Check seasoning and serve.

MARINADES FOR TOUGH BIRDS

Marinades add flavour to meat, and help to tenderize it. This is because most marinades contain an acid such as wine or fruit juice which helps break down tough fibres. Fresh pineapple juice is most effective as it contains a special enzyme that breaks down proteins and tenderizes meat.

- Fresh pineapple juice mixed with grated lemon zest.
- Lemon juice, crushed garlic and dried red pepper flakes.
- Red wine, cranberry juice and juniper berries.
- Orange juice, lime juice, cracked peppercorns, coriander seeds and chopped fresh chilli.
- White wine, cider vinegar, cumin seeds, allspice berries and cinnamon stick.
- Red wine, cinnamon stick and cracked cloves.
- Sherry vinegar, oil, thyme, sage and bay leaf.
- Red wine, rosemary and marjoram.

TERRINES & PATES

Any bone and sinew free poultry or game meat can be ground up turned into a spreadable pâté, or moulded and cooked as a terrine. Don't overcook the meat; pâtés and terrines are at their best when moist and juicy.

CHICKEN LIVER PATE

250 g chicken livers
125 g unsalted butter, softened
2 tbsp brandy
Salt and freshly ground pepper
25–50 g lukewarm liquid clarified
    butter

Toss chicken livers in about one-third of the butter until they change colour, about 5 minutes. Remove from the pan and purée in a food processor with the remaining butter and the brandy. Add seasonings to taste, Transfer the pâté to four ramekins, smooth the surface, then cover with clarified butter. Cool, then chill in the refrigerator. Serves 4.

FARCE FOR RABBIT TERRINE

1.5 kg rabbit
2 shallots, roughly chopped
2 eggs
150 ml double cream
2 tbsp shelled pistachios
1 tbsp dried cranberries
2 tbsp chopped fresh parsley
Freshly grated nutmeg
Salt and freshly ground pepper

Cut up the rabbit (see page 11), then remove the meat from the bones. Set aside the best pieces and mince the rest in a food processor with the shallots. Work in the eggs and cream, then turn the mixture into a bowl and mix in the nuts, dried cranberries, parsley and seasonings to taste.

MAKING A PAN-FRIED LIVER PATE

One of the easiest ways to make a pâté is by pan-frying livers quickly, working them to a fine or coarse purée in a food processor, then chilling until firm in the refrigerator. Chicken livers are favoured because of their mild flavour and soft texture. Take care not to overcook them or they will toughen.

COOKING THE LIVERS
Keep them moving in hot butter in the centre of the pan, so they do not stick or burn, until pink-tinged.

ADDING CLARIFIED BUTTER
Spoon liquid clarified butter over the pâté to keep it airtight – the mixture may discolour in contact with air.

MAKING A RABBIT TERRINE

The technique here is to contrast a creamy, smooth farce with thin slivers of tender meat to make an easy layered terrine. The addition of aspic after baking helps keep the terrine moist. It also gives the terrine a professional-looking finish.

1 Line a 1.5 litre terrine with about 15 rindless streaky bacon rashers. Make sure there are no gaps and allow the ends to overhang.

2 Put half the farce (see box, left) in the terrine, cover with pieces of rabbit in an even layer, then spoon in the remaining farce.

3 Fold over the overhanging rashers, arranging them in an attractive pattern. Cover the mould and bake in a *bain marie* at 180°C for 2 hours.

4 Slowly pour 300–350 ml liquid aspic (see page 35) over the terrine. Add it a little at a time so that it soaks in. Let cool, then refrigerate until set before slicing.

CONSOMME

A clear stock-based soup, consommé is prepared from chicken, beef or veal stock, which is clarified by the addition of egg whites and vegetables. The vegetables also enhance flavour and colour.

MAKING CONSOMME

This easy method of clarifying stock uses a mixture of egg whites, a mirepoix of vegetables (roughly diced carrot, onion and celery) and an acid in the form of lemon juice. Chicken consommé is made here, but the same technique applies to making beef or veal consommé.

1 Whisk 3–4 egg whites with a fork until frothy. Add 2 tbsp lemon juice and about 350 g *mirepoix*.

2 Add the egg mixture to 2 litres warm stock; bring to the boil. Whisk until a crust forms, 4–6 minutes.

3 Make a hole in the crust for the liquid to simmer through. Simmer gently for about 1 hour – do not stir.

4 Line a sieve with damp muslin and hold it over a large bowl. Break the crust and ladle the consommé through the muslin. Reheat in a clean pan and garnish just before serving with a black truffle *julienne* and leaves of fresh chervil, as shown here. Or sprinkle with very finely diced raw vegetables, the traditional garnish.

MAKING ASPIC

Add gelatine to consommé to make aspic that is firm enough to cut decoratively into shapes as a garnish. Liquid aspic is often used to set savoury moulds, mousses and terrines, and for glazing fish, meat and poultry (see page 23).

Soak gelatine leaves for 2–3 minutes in a little of the measured amount of cold consommé (allow 7 g gelatine for every 500 ml liquid). Warm the remaining consommé, then add the gelatine and its soaking liquid. Stir over a gentle heat until the gelatine has melted. Test by chilling 1 tbsp on a saucer.

CHOOSING & USING EGGS

Eggs are one of our most valued and useful ingredients in the kitchen – many recipes simply wouldn't be possible without their aerating, thickening and emulsifying capabilities.

FREE-RANGE

Around 85% of eggs in the UK are produced using the "laying cage system" or battery method. For eggs to be called free-range, the birds must have access to runs and a variety of vegetation, such as grass and corn. Although they have more freedom, these hens are more affected by weather conditions and predators and, as a result, they are a little more expensive.

SHELL COLOURS

The colour of an egg shell is determined by the breed of hen and its diet. The colour can range from speckled (quail's egg) to blue (duck's egg). Hen's eggs, either white or brown, are most commonly used – they taste the same, the difference in colour having no effect on flavour.

Clockwise, from bottom left: duck egg (off-white); duck egg (blue); hen's egg (white); pullet's egg (small brown); hen's egg (brown); quail's egg (small and speckled).

HOW TO TEST FOR FRESHNESS

First check the "best before" date (see Safety First box, opposite page). If there is no date, test the freshness by immersing the egg in water as shown here. As the egg gets older it loses water through the shell, making the air pocket larger – so the older the egg the lighter it will be.

A fresh egg is heavy due to its high water content. It will settle horizontally on the bottom of the glass.

With a less fresh egg the air pockets will expand and make the egg float vertically, tip down, in the water.

An old, stale egg contains too much air and will float to the surface of the water. Do not use the egg.

SEPARATING YOLK FROM WHITE

It is easiest to separate eggs when they are cold – the yolk is firm, and there is less chance that it will run into the white. Whites will not whisk properly if there is any yolk in them.

HAND METHOD
Crack egg into a bowl, then lift it up and cup it in your hand to let all the white drip through your fingers.

SHELL METHOD
Crack egg shell in half. Pass the yolk backwards and forwards between the halves until the white is in the bowl.

SAFETY FIRST

- Use eggs within the "best before" date. Check for the Lion Mark which ensures hygienic production standards greater than those required by UK or EC law.
- Salmonella bacteria can enter eggs through cracks in the shell, so only buy eggs with clean, undamaged shells.
- Wash your hands before and after handling egg shells.
- The elderly, people who are suffering an illness, pregnant women, babies and children are vulnerable to the risk of salmonella. All should avoid eating raw eggs and foods containing them.
- It is important to cook all egg dishes thoroughly – heat destroys salmonella.

TRICK OF THE TRADE

BLENDING ALBUMEN STRANDS

Egg yolk is anchored in the white by thick albumen strands. The strands should be sieved or blended into the whites so that they help to stabilize the foam.

SIEVING
Work the egg white through a fine sieve held over a bowl with a spoon to break up the albumen strands.

BLENDING
Put the egg whites in a bowl and use chopsticks or a fork to lift the whites and break up the albumen strands.

STORING EGGS

- Refrigerate eggs as soon as possible after buying them.
- Store eggs in their carton, away from strong-smelling foods.
- Store eggs pointed-end down to keep the yolks centred.
- Separated whites and yolks or shelled whole eggs should be refrigerated in airtight containers. Whites will keep for 1 week, yolks and whole eggs up to 2 days.
- Use food containing raw eggs within 2 days.
- Hard-boiled eggs in their shells will keep for up to 1 week.

NUTRITIONAL VALUE OF EGGS

Eggs are a valuable source of protein (one large egg contains 12–15% of the recommended daily allowance for an adult), supplying all essential amino acids needed by the body.

They also contain the minerals iron, iodine and calcium and vitamins A, B, D, E and K. Indeed, vitamin C is the only vitamin that is not present in an egg.

Eggs are also low in calories, supplying about 75 calories each. In the past, a limit on the number of eggs consumed per person per week was advised because of the cholesterol content, but more recent research shows that the dietary intake of saturated fat is the main cause of increased blood cholesterol levels. So, despite the fact that an egg contains 213 mg of cholesterol, all of which is within the yolk, the level of saturated fat is very low.

Although egg intake is restricted in some special diets, the current UK dietary guideline for egg consumption for an adult is 2–3 eggs per week.

WHISKING EGG WHITES

To achieve greater volume and stability before whisking egg whites, let them stand at room temperature for about 1 hour in a covered bowl. Whether whisking by hand or machine, make sure all utensils are free of grease and that the bowl is deep enough to hold the volume of whisked whites.

BY HAND

Put whites in a stainless steel or glass bowl. Whisk them from the bottom of the bowl upwards in a circular motion. For greatest volume, use a large balloon whisk.

BY MACHINE

With the whisk attachment of a tabletop electric mixer, start whisking slowly, to break up the whites, then increase the speed as they thicken. A little salt relaxes the albumen and makes whisking easier.

MAKING EGG WASH

A mixture of egg yolk and water is brushed over bread or pastry before baking to give a rich, golden colour and a glossy glaze.

Mix 1 egg yolk with 1 tbsp water and a pinch of salt. Whisk with a fork until combined. Brush the egg wash over bread or pastry with a pastry brush just before baking.

COOKING EGGS

The art of cooking a perfect egg is simple – once you know how.
The techniques shown here may seem very basic, but they are an
essential part of every good cook's repertoire.

BOILING

Some cooks put eggs in cold water to start, others in hot. The hot-water method shown here is best for accurate timing. Always use fresh eggs at room temperature – the shells of eggs taken straight from the refrigerator are more likely to crack.

1 Put the eggs in a pan of gently bubbling water and add a pinch of salt. Start timing from the moment the water returns to the boil.

2 For soft-boiled eggs, simmer gently for 3–4 minutes. Remove with a slotted spoon and cut off the tops with a knife.

3 Remove the top part of the shell and any small pieces that have fallen into the egg. The white should be just set, the yolk runny.

HARD-BOILED
Simmer for 6–10 minutes. Plunge immediately into cold water, to prevent greying around the yolk, then peel.

TRICK OF THE TRADE

CAVIAR EGGS
For an elegant breakfast or brunch, serve soft-boiled eggs Russian-style.

Soft-boil the eggs and cut off the tops following the directions above, then spoon in a little caviar, or red lumpfish roe as shown here.

POACHING

Very fresh eggs and a wide, shallow pan are essential for successful poaching. For accurate timing, cook no more than four eggs at a time.

Add 1 tbsp wine vinegar and a tarragon sprig to boiling water. Do not add salt. Turn off the heat, crack in the eggs and cover. Let stand until the whites are opaque, 3 minutes.

BAKING

It's tricky to get the whites set and the yolks runny at the same time when baking eggs. Here are two methods, the classic French oeufs en cocotte *and the more unusual Mexican* huevos rancheros. *Stand the dishes on paper towels when baking in a bain marie, to prevent overcooking and cracking the china.*

OEUFS EN COCOTTE
Put eggs in buttered ramekins and add 2 tbsp cream and seasonings to each one. Cover and bake in a *bain marie* at 180°C for 6–8 minutes.

HUEVOS RANCHEROS
Put cooked sliced peppers and onions in individual gratin dishes. Top each with an egg. Cover and bake at 180°C for 8–12 minutes. Top with *salsa*.

SCRAMBLING

The secret of making perfect, creamy-textured scrambled eggs is to cook them over a low heat and patiently stir them all the time. Never attempt to rush scrambled eggs or they will be stiff and rubbery. For two servings, allow 4 eggs, 2 tbsp cream or milk and seasonings to taste.

1 Put the eggs in a jug with the cream or milk and salt and pepper to taste. Whisk with a fork for 1 minute. The seasoning prevents streaking.

2 Heat enough butter to coat the bottom of a frying pan. When the butter is foaming, pour in the egg mixture.

3 Stir constantly with a wooden spoon over a low heat for 5–8 minutes, then stir for 1–2 minutes off the heat. Serve immediately.

ADDITIONS TO SCRAMBLED EGGS

Many ingredients can be whisked into eggs before they are scrambled or while cooking to add texture and flavour.

- In the Basque dish *pipérade*, onions, peppers and mushrooms are fried, then the eggs are stirred in. Alternatives include chopped ham or pesto.
- One famous dish, Hangtown Fry, originated during the 1849 gold rush in California. It combines deep-fried breaded oysters with scrambled eggs.
- The Chinese make a dish called "red, green and yellow" – cubes of tomato and cucumber mixed with scrambled eggs.

SHALLOW-FRYING

For most people, the perfect fried egg has a runny yolk and a set white. There are two ways of achieving this – by keeping the egg yolk "sunny-side up" during frying and basting it with hot fat, or by turning it "over easy" halfway through. This second method is less popular because the yolk can easily be broken during turning, and it loses its bright yellow colour.

DEEP-FRYING

This French technique is often used for eggs that are to be served on croûtes. Olive oil gives a delicious flavour, but other oils can be used. Butter is not suitable – it will burn.

DEEP-FRIED EGGS ESCOFFIER STYLE

4 tomatoes, halved
Salt and freshly ground pepper
4 tbsp fresh white breadcrumbs
1 tbsp chopped fresh parsley
1 shallot, finely chopped
4 eggs

Place tomatoes, cut-side up, in a baking dish and season well. Mix together the breadcrumbs, parsley and shallot and spoon over the tomatoes. Bake at 180°C for 10 minutes. Deep-fry the eggs (see left) and serve on warmed plates the tomato halves alongside. Serves 4.

SUNNY-SIDE UP
Heat a shallow layer of oil or butter in a frying pan until hot but not smoking. Add the eggs and fry over a moderate heat, basting constantly with the hot fat, for 3–4 minutes. Baste the white only to keep the yolk runny, or the white and the yolk, as you like.

NEATLY-SHAPED EGGS
Coat the bottom of a frying pan with oil, then place a metal pastry cutter (stainless steel is preferable) in the pan and heat until hot. Slide the egg into the cutter and fry as for sunny-side up eggs (see left). Remove cutter carefully before removing the egg.

Heat about 2 cm oil in a deep frying pan until it is very hot but not smoking. Add 1 egg, spoon the hot oil over it and fold the white over the yolk to enclose it. Cook for 1 minute. Remove the egg with a slotted spoon and drain on paper towels. Repeat with more eggs.

OMELETTES

In classic French cuisine, an omelette is a folded, fluffy creation, simply made by whisking eggs and cooking them quickly in a traditional pan. In other parts of the world, however, an omelette is quite a different thing.

FLAVOURINGS FOR OMELETTES

Add flavourings to the egg mixture before cooking or spoon fillings into the centre of the omelette and fold over to enclose. The following combinations are delicious.

- Grated cheese and finely diced tomatoes.
- Snipped bacon sautéed in walnut oil until crisp with fresh spinach leaves.
- Sliced or diced peppers and shallots sautéed in butter with sliced mushrooms.
- Smoked salmon shavings and a little fresh dill.
- Chunks of cooked sausage and caramelized onion slices.
- Strips of smoked ham and blanched asparagus tips.

MAKING A FOLDED OMELETTE

This is the classic French omelette which is traditionally cooked in a well-seasoned cast-iron pan, although here a non-stick frying pan serves the same purpose. For best results, allow 15 g butter and 3 eggs per omelette in a 20-cm pan.

1 Immediately before cooking, lightly beat the eggs and seasonings with a fork. Do not overbeat the mixture or the finished omelette will be stiff.

2 Heat the butter over a high heat until foaming. Pour in the eggs. Mix with a fork for even distribution.

3 Cook quickly, drawing in the edges with a fork to allow the uncooked egg to run underneath.

4 Tilt the pan and fold the omelette over towards one side of the pan, pushing it with the fork to help it roll.

MAKING A JAPANESE OMELETTE

Japanese omelettes offer a symmetrical shape and light texture. They are traditionally made in a 20-cm square pan, and they are rolled as they are fried. If you do not have a pan of this shape, use a round pan and trim the sides of the omelette once cooked. Allow 1 egg and 2 tbsp water for each omelette; the addition of water thins the batter to create light texture. Serve cut into slices or shreds (see opposite page).

1 Brush the pan with a little oil and heat. Pour in half the egg mixture. Tilt the pan to make an even layer. As surface bubbles appear, loosen the edges with a palette knife.

2 Roll omelette towards you with chopsticks. Cook until set, about 1 minute. Make another omelette with remaining mixture.

MAKING OMELETTE SHREDS

In Asian cooking, shreds made from very thin omelettes are used as toppings and garnishes. For a dish to serve four, use 1 egg beaten with a pinch of salt. Cook the omelette in a wok.

1 Heat 1 tbsp oil. Swirl in egg. Cook over moderate heat for 1–2 minutes.

2 Slide the omelette out of the wok, roll up and let cool. Shred crosswise.

MAKING A SOUFFLE OMELETTE

This type of omelette is made by separating eggs, beating the whites until stiff, then folding them into the yolks. As its name suggests, the finished omelette is therefore lighter and fluffier than a conventional omelette. In classic French cuisine, soufflé omelettes are often sweet, and the yolks are beaten to the ribbon stage with sugar before the whites are folded in.

Whisk 3 egg whites until stiff. Fold into 3 seasoned and whisked yolks. Cook as for a folded omelette (see opposite page), without mixing with a fork in step 2.

MAKING AN EGGAH

A traditional Persian dish, an eggah is a kind of thick, firm omelette baked in the oven and served sliced or cut into wedges, hot or cold. Eggahs can be made plain, with a touch of spice, but adding other ingredients is more traditional. Chopped spinach is used here, but fresh herbs, onion, garlic, peppers or other vegetables may be used.

1 Mix 6 beaten eggs with chosen flavourings. Pour into an oiled baking dish.

2 Bake at 170°C until firm, 15–20 minutes. Cut into wedges to serve.

SPANISH TORTILLAS

This omelette is similar to an Italian *frittata*, except for the cooking technique and some of the flavourings used. Onions and potatoes are fried in a generous amount of olive oil, then beaten eggs are added. Unlike *frittata*, which is finished by browning under the grill, a *tortilla* is always flipped over in the pan to brown and set both sides.

MAKING A FRITTATA

A thick, flat Italian omelette, a frittata *is partially cooked on top of the stove in a heavy-based pan, then grilled until brown and set. For a 30-cm* frittata, *use 1–2 tbsp olive oil, 7–10 eggs and flavourings of your choice. The chopped peppers illustrated here are traditional, so too are asparagus, globe artichokes, sliced green beans, mixed chopped herbs, grated Parmesan, tomatoes, chopped onions and garlic.*

Whisk eggs with flavourings and pour into hot olive oil. Cook for 15 minutes over a low heat, then brown under the grill for 1–2 minutes.

Cheese Soufflés

These light-as-air cheese puffs are rightly called soufflés, despite their unconventional sabayon-type base. They are served floating on a rich cheese cream, called a fondue *after the French word for melt.*

SERVES 4

4 eggs, separated

100 ml dry white wine

Salt and freshly ground pepper

100 g Parmesan cheese, freshly grated

FOR THE FONDUE

200 ml double cream

100 g Gruyère or other easy-melting cheese, grated

TO SERVE

Snipped chives

Freshly grated Parmesan cheese

Put the egg yolks and wine in a large heatproof bowl set over a pan of gently simmering water (bain marie) and whisk them together until they reach the ribbon stage. Remove the bowl from the bain marie and whisk until the mixture is cool.

In another bowl, whisk the egg whites until stiff. Fold the whites gently but thoroughly into the egg yolk mixture and add salt and pepper to taste.

Bring the cream to the boil in a pan and stir in the Gruyère until melted and smooth. Pour into four shallow ovenproof dishes.

Using two spoons, shape the egg mixture into quenelles (small dumplings) and float on the fondue. Sprinkle each quenelle with one-quarter of the grated Parmesan. Bake at 180°C for 10 minutes or until the soufflés are puffed up and golden brown. Serve at once, sprinkled with snipped chives, with grated Parmesan cheese handed separately.

> ### ALTERNATIVE FLAVOURINGS
>
> - Replace the Gruyère with blue cheese.
> - Add a little ready-made *rouille* to the fondue.
> - Add freshly chopped herbs to the fondue.

Making a Soufflé

Soufflés have a light, fluffy texture due to the incorporation of air. Here, a standard whisk is used over a bain marie; for even greater volume, use a large balloon whisk or a hand-held electric mixer. The bowl for the egg whites must be spotlessly clean or they will not whisk.

Whisk the egg yolks with the wine until the mixture is pale and thick enough to leave a ribbon trail when lifted.

Whisk the egg whites at a steady pace to a white foam that will hold a stiff peak.

Fold together using a scooping and cutting action to ensure you lose as little of the whisked-in air as possible.

USING HERBS & SPICES

An invaluable addition to the kitchen, fresh herbs and aromatic spices give dishes distinctive taste and ethnic personality. These charts help pair flavourings with the foods they best enhance.

STORING HERBS

Because they do not keep well, fresh herbs are best used straight after picking. The following methods of storage will help keep them fresh and prolong their life, essential techniques in the summer months if you have a herb garden.

- For short storage of 1-2 days, pack freshly picked herbs in plastic bags in the refrigerator. Delicate varieties, such as basil, benefit from being wrapped in slightly damp paper towels before they are placed in bags.
- To dry herbs, hang them up by their stalks in a dry, well-ventilated room. This position concentrates the flavour in the leaves. Once dried, store herbs in airtight containers.
- Fresh herbs can be frozen with excellent results. For best flavour, use young herbs picked before the flowering stage. Gather them in the early morning when the dew has dried and the leaves are at their most aromatic. Strip off the leaves and chop them finely (bay, rosemary, sage and thyme should not be chopped, but snipped into small sprigs). Place chopped herbs in ice-cube trays, cover with iced water and freeze. When solid, pack herb ice cubes in freezer bags, ready to drop into liquids straight from the freezer. Sprigs of herbs should be frozen as they are, in airtight containers.

HERBS AND THEIR USES

	FLAVOUR	USE WITH
BASIL	*Sweet, warm, softly spicy, aromatic*	White fish, veal, chicken, seafood, salad greens, eggs, tomatoes, pesto and other pasta sauces
BAY	*Aromatic, pungent*	Soups, stocks, stews, casseroles, sauces (especially béchamel)
CHERVIL	*Delicate, slightly anise-like*	Fish, chicken, omelettes, sauces
CHIVES	*Mild, oniony*	Fish, eggs, cheese, salads, creamy soups, potatoes
CORIANDER	*Intensely aromatic, spicy*	Asian, Middle Eastern and Mexican dishes, carrots, salads, yogurt
CURRY LEAVES	*Spicy "curry" flavour*	Indian curries, casseroles, soups, seafood, stuffings
DILL	*Delicate, anise-like*	Salmon, soused herring, veal, carrots, cucumbers, potatoes, mayonnaise, soured cream, soft fresh cheeses
FENNEL	*Anise-like*	Fish soups, pork, seafood, eggs
MARJORAM/ OREGANO	*Sweet, aromatic, pungent*	Grilled meats, chicken, tomato sauces, eggs. cheese, flavoured oils and marinades
MINT	*Strong, sweet, clean*	Cucumber, potatoes, peas, cheese, melon, chilled soups, lamb, yogurt
PARSLEY	*Fresh, slightly spicy*	Eggs, fish, soups, poultry, meat
ROSEMARY	*Pungent, oily, aromatic*	Lamb, chicken, pork, bread, potatoes
SAGE	*Aromatic, slightly bitter*	Pork, veal, duck, goose, turkey, pulses, eggs, ricotta, Parmesan cheese, risotto, pasta
SUMMER SAVORY	*Pungent, lemony*	Pulses, broad and French beans, eggs, cheese, grilled meats, tomato sauce
TARRAGON	*Aromatic, anise-like, cooling*	Chicken, eggs, tomatoes, béarnaise
THYME	*Intensely aromatic*	Poultry and meat roasts and casseroles, roast potatoes

SPICES AND THEIR USES

	FLAVOUR	FORM	USE WITH
ALLSPICE	*Hints of clove and cinnamon*	Whole berries or ground	Caribbean meat stews, game, lamb, onions, cabbage, spiced vinegar, poached fruits, cakes, breads, and pies
CARAWAY	*Aromatic, strong hints of fennel*	Whole seeds or ground	Meat stews, sausages, cabbage, pork, sauerkraut, breads, cheese, rich fruit cakes
CARDAMOM	*Pungent, lemony*	Pods, loose seeds or ground	Indian and Middle Eastern curries, stews, pickling brines, pastries, cakes, fruit dishes, quick breads
CAYENNE/ CHILLI POWDER	*Spicy, very hot*	Ground	Indian, Mexican, Cajun, Caribbean and Creole dishes, seafood, béarnaise sauce
CINNAMON	*Sweet, warm aromatic*	Sticks or ground	Middle-Eastern dishes, curries, fruit desserts, cakes and breads, milk and rice puddings, chocolate desserts
CLOVES	*Sweet, strong*	Whole buds or ground	Ham and pork, sweet potatoes, pumpkin, spiced cakes, apples and other fruits, stocks
CORIANDER	*Fragrant, lemony*	Whole berries or ground	Indian and Oriental dishes, meat, chicken, pickled fish, mushrooms, breads, cakes, pastries and custards
CUMIN	*Pungent, warm, earthy*	Whole seeds or ground	Indian and Mexican dishes, pork, chicken, lamb, cheese, bean soups, rice pilafs
FENNEL SEED		Sweet, licquorice-flavoured	Mediterranean fish soups and stews, grilled fish
GINGER	*Pungent, spicy*	Fresh root or ground	Oriental and Indian dishes, chicken, vegetables, particularly pumpkin and carrots, fruits such as melon and rhubarb, cakes and biscuits
JUNIPER	*Pungent, clean, pine-scented*	Berries	Sausage, pork and game dishes, pâtés and terrines, particularly venison, cabbage, stuffings
MACE	*Sweet, fragrant*	Whole blades or ground	As for nutmeg
MUSTARD	*Pungent, hot*	Whole seeds or ground	Beef and pork, chicken, rabbit, vegetables, pickles and relishes, sauces and dressings
NUTMEG	*Sweet, fragrant*	Whole or ground	Stuffed pastas, meat and béchamel sauces, spinach and potato gratins, cakes and biscuits, milk puddings and custards, mulled wine
PAPRIKA	*Pungent, sweet or hot*	Ground	Meat and poultry, especially Eastern European dishes, eggs, vegetables, cream cheese
PEPPER	*Pungent, mild or hot*	Berries (peppercorns) or ground	Almost every savoury dish and a few sweet ones, such as strawberries and sorbets
POPPY SEEDS	*Nutty, sweet*	Whole and ground	Breads, cakes, pastries, salads, coleslaws, egg noodles, sauces for meat and fish
STAR ANISE	*Warm, aromatic, spicy-sweet*	Whole, broken, seeds and ground	Oriental-style dishes, especially Chinese, pork, duck and chicken, fish and shellfish dishes, marinades
TURMERIC	*Warm, mild aroma*	Whole and ground	Adds subtle flavouring and a distinctive yellow colour, used in curry powders, rice, pulse dishes and chutneys

MEASUREMENT CHARTS

Accurate measurements are crucial to the success of any dish. The following charts give quick and easy reference for gauging oven temperatures and converting metric and imperial units for ingredients and equipment.

OVEN TEMPERATURES

CELSIUS	FAHRENHEIT	GAS	DESCRIPTION
110°C	225°F	¼	Cool
120°C	250°F	½	Cool
140°C	275°F	1	Very low
150°C	300°F	2	Very low
160°C	325°F	3	Low
170°C	325°F	3	Moderate
180°C	350°F	4	Moderate
190°C	375°F	5	Moderately hot
200°C	400°F	6	Hot
220°C	425°F	7	Hot
230°C	450°F	8	Very hot

US CUPS

CUPS	METRIC
¼ cup	60 ml
⅓ cup	70 ml
½ cup	125 ml
⅔ cup	150 ml
¾ cup	175 ml
1 cup	250 ml
1½ cups	375 ml
2 cups	500 ml
3 cups	750 ml
4 cups	1 litre
6 cups	1.5 litres

SPOONS

METRIC	IMPERIAL
1.25 ml	¼ tsp
2.5 ml	½ tsp
5 ml	1 tsp
10 ml	2 tsp
15 ml	3 tsp/1 tbsp
30 ml	2 tbsp
45 ml	3 tbsp
60 ml	4 tbsp
75 ml	5 tbsp
90 ml	6 tbsp

VOLUME

METRIC	IMPERIAL	METRIC	IMPERIAL	METRIC	IMPERIAL
25 ml	1 fl oz	300 ml	10 fl oz/½ pint	1 litre	1¾ pints
50 ml	2 fl oz	350 ml	12 fl oz	1.2 litres	2 pints
75 ml	2½ fl oz	400 ml	14 fl oz	1.3 litres	2¼ pints
100 ml	3½ fl oz	425 ml	15 fl oz/¾ pint	1.4 litres	2½ pints
125 ml	4 fl oz	450 ml	16 fl oz	1.5 litres	2¾ pints
150 ml	5 fl oz/¼ pint	500 ml	18 fl oz	1.7 litres	3 pints
175 ml	6 fl oz	568 ml	20 fl oz/1 pint	2 litres	3½ pints
200 ml	7 fl oz/⅓ pint	600 ml	1 pint milk	2.5 litres	4½ pints
225 ml	8 fl oz	700 ml	1¼ pints	2.8 litres	5 pints
250 ml	9 fl oz	850 ml	1½ pints	3 litres	5¼ pints

WEIGHT

METRIC	IMPERIAL	METRIC	IMPERIAL
5 g	⅛ oz	325 g	11½ oz
10 g	¼ oz	350 g	12 oz
15 g	½ oz	375 g	13 oz
20 g	¾ oz	400 g	14 oz
25 g	1 oz	425 g	15 oz
35 g	1¼ oz	450 g	1 lb
40 g	1½ oz	500 g	1 lb 2 oz
50 g	1¾ oz	550 g	1 lb 4 oz
55 g	2 oz	600 g	1 lb 5 oz
60 g	2¼ oz	650 g	1 lb 7 oz
70 g	2½ oz	700 g	1 lb 9 oz
75 g	2¾ oz	750 g	1 lb 10 oz
85 g	3 oz	800 g	1 lb 12 oz
90 g	3¼ oz	850 g	1 lb 14 oz
100 g	3½ oz	900 g	2 lb
115 g	4 oz	950 g	2 lb 2 oz
125 g	4½ oz	1 kg	2 lb 4 oz
140 g	5 oz	1.25 kg	2 lb 12 oz
150 g	5½ oz	1.3 kg	3 lb
175 g	6 oz	1.5 kg	3 lb 5 oz
200 g	7 oz	1.6 kg	3 lb 8 oz
225 g	8 oz	1.8 kg	4 lb
250 g	9 oz	2 kg	4 lb 8 oz
275 g	9¾ oz	2.25 kg	5 lb
280 g	10 oz	2.5 kg	5 lb 8 oz
300 g	10½ oz	2.7 kg	6 lb
315 g	11 oz	3 kg	6 lb 8 oz

LINEAR MEASUREMENTS

METRIC	IMPERIAL	METRIC	IMPERIAL
2 mm	1/16 in	17 cm	6½ in
3 mm	⅛ in	18 cm	7 in
5 mm	¼ in	19 cm	7½ in
8 mm	⅜ in	20 cm	8 in
10 mm/1 cm	½ in	22 cm	8½ in
1.5 cm	⅝ in	23 cm	9 in
2 cm	¾ in	24 cm	9½ in
2.5 cm	1 in	25 cm	10 in
3 cm	1¼ in	26 cm	10½ in
4 cm	1½ in	27 cm	10¾ in
4.5 cm	1¾ in	28 cm	11 in
5 cm	2 in	29 cm	11½ in
5.5 cm	2¼ in	30 cm	12 in
6 cm	2½ in	31 cm	12½ in
7 cm	2¾ in	33 cm	13 in
7.5 cm	3 in	34 cm	13½ in
8 cm	3¼ in	35 cm	14 in
9 cm	3½ in	37 cm	14½ in
9.5 cm	3¾ in	38 cm	15 in
10 cm	4 in	39 cm	15½ in
11 cm	4¼ in	40 cm	16 in
12 cm	4½ in	42 cm	16½ in
12.5 cm	4¾ in	43 cm	17 in
13 cm	5 in	44 cm	17½ in
14 cm	5½ in	46 cm	18 in
15 cm	6 in	48 cm	19 in
16 cm	6¼ in	50 cm	20 in

INDEX